THE
ARTILLERY COMPANY OF NEWPORT

(a pictorial history)

Fiat Justitia Ruat Coelum
Let Justice Prevail Though The Heavens May Fall

Members of the Artillery Company of Newport turn out in uniforms of the wars fought since the unit was chartered in 1741.

THE
ARTILLERY COMPANY
OF
NEWPORT

(A Pictorial History)

Walter K. Schroder

HERITAGE BOOKS
2014

HERITAGE BOOKS

AN IMPRINT OF HERITAGE BOOKS, INC.

Books, CDs, and more—Worldwide

For our listing of thousands of titles see our website
at
www.HeritageBooks.com

Published 2014 by
HERITAGE BOOKS, INC.
Publishing Division
5810 Ruatan Street
Berwyn Heights, Md. 20740

Heritage Books by the author:

Stars and Swastikas: The Boy Who Wore Two Uniforms: Expanded Edition
The Artillery Company of Newport: A Pictorial History
The Hessian Drummer Boy of Newport
The Hessian Occupation of Newport and Rhode Island, 1776–1779

Cover design by The Jamestown Press

International Standard Book Numbers
Paperbound: 978-0-7884-5526-1
Clothbound: 978-0-7884-9056-9

*Dedicated to the men and women who
faithfully uphold the
traditions of the Artillery Company of Newport*

The Field Artillery Song

(by General Edmund Gruber)

Over hill, over dale, we have
hit the dusty trail,
And those Caissons Go Rolling
Along---
"Counter march! Right about!"
Hear those wagon soldiers
shout,
While those Caissons go Rolling
Along.

Chorus

For its "Hi! Hi! Hee!"in the
Field Artillery,
Call off your numbers loud and
strong---
And where-e'er we go, You will
always know
That those Caissons are Rolling Along
(Keep 'em rolling)
That those Caissons are Rolling
Along.

Table of Contents

Preface   IX

Introduction   XI

Formation and Charter   1

The Armory   7

The Museum   23

Calls to Duty   41

Historical Functions   57

Honors, Social Functions & Parades   73

Personages   85

APPENDIX

I   Charter of 1741   98

II   List of Colonels Commanding   100

III   Revitalized Charter of 1792   101

IV   Important Dates   102

References   103

Other Books by the Author   104

The Author   105

Preface

Parades and other military demonstrations generally attract the public for the precision exercises and colorful military attire of the marchers, particularly when such activities commemorate local and national historic events. At times the sounds of bands combined with the thunder of cannon fire add to the festive or solemn nature of the occasion.

The Artillery Company of Newport, established under a Charter granted by the General Assembly of the British Colony of Rhode Island in 1741, is the oldest Militia unit in Rhode Island operating under its original Charter. It can often be seen dressed in colonial attire while participating in a variety of commemorative, and of late also privately sponsored celebrations.

The Artillery Company of Newport has been, and to this day still is a 'must see' to the enthusiastic. Their appearance in public has for decades been taken for granted. However, despite people's attraction to these public appearances, there are many who are unaware that the Artillery Company of Newport also maintains an armory and museum in the downtown historic district of the City of Newport, Rhode Island that is open to public visitation. Impressive exhibits of weaponry, military artifacts and uniforms range from the time the Charter came into being, thru the wars and the many military engagements in which Americans, including Newporters, participated in to this very day. For a quick course in Rhode Island Military History, one need only visit the home of the Artillery Company of Newport on Clarke Street.

This photographic collection has been compiled to serve as a guide to the history and holdings of the armory and museum, and to provide an insight for public appreciation of the service the all-volunteer Artillery Company of Newport has, and is still, providing to the City of Newport and the State of Rhode Island.

This work could not have been completed without the direct commitment of the Artillery Company by granting access to their holdings, and the dedicated assistance provided by some of its members who volunteered their time as well as personal records and photographs for inclusion in this compilation of historical data.

Of particular note was the commitment of Robert S. Edenbach, the present Colonel Commanding of the Artillery Company of Newport, for supporting this undertaking, and of his Curator, Ron Jones, for assisting me in securing and identifying materials of interest to the project over a period of many months, hereafter identified as (ACN files). A very special 'thank you' to Colonel Roy Lauth for making available his extensive family archives (LFA) of photos and ephemera compiled and meticulously maintained over many decades by his mother, Mrs. Ruth Lauth.

A number of company members and friends contributed photos and written matter, or participated in the photography effort for the book. I wish to thank them individually and collectively for their cooperation and interest in the success of this project. They include in particular:

Colonel Robert Edenbach (RE), Curator Ron Jones (RJ), Brian Pelletier, (BP), David Dewhurst (DD), Kenneth Pike (ACN Web), ACN Photographer Tom Donnelly (TD), John Duchesneau (JD), and Stephen Fasano (SF), Professional Photographer. Advice offered by Bert Lippincott, Newport Historical Society, and James Brady is sincerely appreciated.

A very special word of thanks to Jeffrey McDonough, Publisher of the Jamestown Press, for taking on the job of editing the manuscript, and to Kimberly Taylor, Production Manager at the Jamestown Press, for her excellent work in formatting the layout of this, my latest undertaking.

Last, but not least I appreciate my wife Lora's patience and tolerance for allowing me to take away from our 'quality time,' the many hours needed to assemble and compile the materials for this project.

— **Walter K. Schroder**

Introduction

Chartered on February 1, 1741, by the General Assembly of the British Colony of Rhode Island and Providence Plantations, the Artillery Company of Newport today has the distinction of being the oldest military unit in Rhode Island operating under its original Charter. To clarify: after a period of inaction following the American War of Independence, the Rhode Island Legislature saw fit in 1792, to revive and declare as good, the original Charter in response to a plea by members of the Company that the unit dispersed in December 1776 following arrival of a British fleet in Newport, and that it is the desire of its members to revive the existence of the Company under the scope of its original Charter, a key element being, that the members periodically elect their own officers.

For many years, the Artillery Company of Newport was an active participant and supplier of manpower in the military conflicts and actions of the 19th and 20th centuries. Operating with an authorized complement of up to 100 men, the Company in the early years manned Fort George and other defensive works in the Newport area.

In 1757, the General Assembly of the Colony authorized one fourth of the Company to support the British in the French and Indian War. This detail participated in an expedition to Crown Point/Fort William Henry, representing the first time members of the Company served beyond the borders of the Colony.

Two members of the Governor's Council ordered the Company to fire upon HMS St. John in 1764 when it attempted to leave Narragansett Bay after two crew members had stolen some chickens and hogs from townsfolk. Looking back, this may have been one of the first acts of armed resistance against King George, their sovereign. This was followed by the Boston Tea Party in 1773 and a general rebellion that resulted from armed encounters at Lexington and Concord.

In early December 1776, when a British armada of seventy transports protected by seven ships of the line and four frigates landed some 6,500 British and Hessian soldiers in Newport, half of the Company left for the mainland to serve with rebel forces, while the remaining members of the unit joined the loyalists in Newport. Even though the Company effectively broke up as a result of this action, its original Charter was revived and reconfirmed by the State Legislature after the American Revolution in 1792, making the Company "the oldest active military company operating under its original charter."

In 1812, the Company dispatched several of its men to assist Oliver Hazard Perry at Lake Erie, in preparing his expedition to Put-In-Bay.

Finally, in 1835 the Company was in a position to build an armory on land donated by Audley Clarke. This provided for the first time a permanent home in Newport for the Company. The Company distinguished itself during the Dorr Rebellion in 1842 for which it was given the right to serve as an independent unit of the Militia and position itself permanently thereafter on the right of the line of assault.

When President Lincoln sought to raise 75,000 volunteers in 1861, to help put down rebellious elements, the Artillery Company quickly increased its strength and enlisted in Providence, as Company "F", of the First Regiment of the Rhode Island Detached Militia. The unit fought in the first Battle of Bull Run, where four of its men lost their lives.

During the Spanish-American War in 1898, a detail of Artillery Company personnel manned the guns at Fort Adams. The Company was given an opportunity to join the newly established National Guard in 1908 with its officers being promoted based on ability and other factors. The Artillery Company of Newport declined the invitation so as not to lose its identity and to maintain its unique status under the Charter of 1741, in particular so as not to lose the right to elect its own officers periodically. Nevertheless, the Company volunteered in 1917, to serve as a unit when the First World War began. However, the government would have accepted the unit if it agreed to serve under federal officers. The Artillery Company withdrew its offer and some of the men detached to serve with federal units. Others served at home, guarding bridges and patrolling beaches on Aquidneck Island.

During subsequent wars, such as World War II, Korea, Vietnam, Iraq and Afghanistan, individual members of the Artillery Company volunteered to serve with federal troops abroad.

Chapter 1

1. Formation and Charter

King Charles II of Britain issued a Charter for his Rhode Island colony that provided for a Governor, Deputy and 10 Assistants (General Assembly). The Legislature held annual elections, granted commissions and was enabled to raise a militia as the colony operated with near autonomy within the Empire and with self government within the colony.

When Britain and Spain went to war in 1740, the people of Newport, anticipating raids from Spanish ships, gave serious thought to the defense of their town. At that time, eighteen of its leading citizens petitioned the General Assembly of His Majesty's Colony of Rhode Island and Providence Plantations for authorization to form a military company. On February 1st, 1741, a Charter for the formation of the Artillery Company of Newport, comprising a complement of one hundred officers and men was formally granted. The unit was formed and equipped, cannon purchased and mounted, and a permanent council of war established.

Richard Ward, of Newport was the 22nd Governor of Rhode Island and Providence Plantations during the period 1740 - 1743, when the Charter was first granted. He had been preceded by Governor John Wanton, also of Newport, who died in office in July 1740.

RI Archives

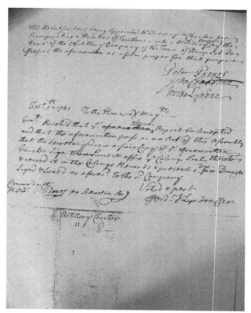

On February 5th, 1741, it was resolved that the Secretary draw up a fair copy of the Charter as written, that he sign the same and affix the Colony's seal thereto, record it in the Colony's Records and present a "fair draught" signed and sealed to the Company.

The original Charter of the Artillery Company of Newport was lost in an Armory fire in 1906. However, the original file box and a copy of the Charter are on display at the company's museum on Clarke Street, Newport, where a larger version of the charter is also on display. See Appendix 1 for a clear text of the document.

Members of the Company were issued a small red booklet containing copies of their Charter and several subsequent amendments. The cover is inscribed with the unit motto:
Fiat Justitia, Ruat Coelum
Let Justice Prevail Though The Heavens May Fall

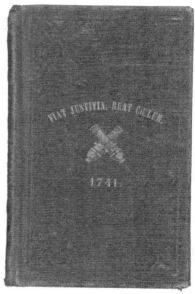

ACN

The first election of officers appears to have been held in April, 1744, when Jahleel Brenton was picked to be captain, John Brown, first lieutenant, John Gidley, second lieutenant; William Mumford, ensign, and Joshua Lyndon, clerk. The rolls of the officers elected over the years show most to have been responsible citizens and leaders in the community who travelled in business, social and political circles, some being considered the most prominent men in town. (For a listing of the Commanding Officers thru to present date, see Appendix II).

The company was in active service until 1776, when the British took possession of Aquidneck Island and Newport. Although the company did not participate in the Revolution as a unit, some members chose to leave the island to join the Continental Army; others stayed on in Newport.

Little information exists that documents the early years following the end of the American Revolution in Newport as relates to activities of the Artillery Company. However, in 1790, despite a prolonged period of inactivity, the company mustered to provide a guard of honor for General George Washington when he visited Newport. Subsequently, on July 9th, 1792, an effort was initiated by some 80 responsible citizens seeking to revive the company. Soon after, the General Assembly granted the petition and on August 9th, 1792, declared the original charter as 'good', thus reviving it as originally written. (See Appendix III). This action insured for the future the existence of the company under its original guidelines and perpetuated its right to continue to 'elect' its officers.

Charter of the ARTILLERY COMPANY OF NEWPORT – *1 February 1741*

At a General Assembly of his Majesty's Colony of Rhode Island and Providence Plantations, in New England, held by adjournment at South Kingstown, within and for the Colony aforesaid, on the first Monday in February, being the first day of said month, in the fifteenth year of his Majesty's reign, George the Second, King of Great Britain, &c., annoque Domini 1741 : –

Whereas the preservation of this Colony, in time of war, depends, under God, chiefly upon the military skill and discipline of the inhabitants; and it being necessary, in order to revive and perpetuate the same, to form and establish a Military Company, which by acquainting and accustoming themselves to the military exercises, by more frequent trainings than the body of the people can attend – may serve for a nursery of skilful Officers, and, in time of an actual invasion, by their superior skill and experience, may render the whole Militia more useful and effectual; –

And Whereas a number of the principal inhabitants of the town of Newport – viz., Jahleel Brenton, Godfrey Malbone, Samuel Wickham, Henry Collins, John Gidley, James Honeyman, jun., John Brown, Nathaniel Coddington, jun., Peleg Brown, Charles Bardin, Simon Pease, David Cheeseborough, Philip Wilkinson, John Freebody, jun., Thomas Wickham, Walter Cranston, Sueton Grant, and William Vernon – have freely offered themselves to begin, and with such others as shall be added to them, to form such a Company; and, by their humble Petition, have prayed this Assembly to grant them a Charter, with such privileges and under such restrictions and limitations as the Assembly shall think proper, –

Wherefore this Assembly, for the reasons and considerations aforesaid, and in order that all due encouragement may be given to the laudable and useful design of the Petitioners, have ordained, constituted, and granted, and by these presents do ordain, constitute, and grant, that they – the said Petitioners, Jahleel Brenton, Godfrey Malbone, Samuel Wickham, Henry Collins, John Gidley, James Honeyman, jun., John Brown, Nathaniel Coddington, jun., Peleg Brown, Charles Bardin, Simon Pease, David Cheeseborough, Philip Wilkinson, John Freebody, jun., Thomas Wickham, Walter Cranston, Sueton Grant, and William Vernon, together with such others as shall be hereafter added to them (not exceeding the number of one hundred in the whole, Officers included) – be; and they are hereby declared to be, a Military Company, by the name of the Artillery Company of the Town of Newport; and by that name they shall have perpetual succession, and shall have and enjoy all the rights, powers, and privileges in this grant, hereafter mentioned : –

1st, It is granted unto said Company, that they, or the greater number of them, shall and may, once in every year (that is to say, on the last Tuesday in April), meet and assemble themselves together, in some convenient place by them appointed, then and there to choose their own officers, viz. one Captain, two Lieutenants, one Ensign, and all other officers necessary for the training, disciplining, and well-ordering of the said Company, at which election no officer shall be chosen but by the greater number of voters then present; the Captain, Lieutenants, and Ensign to be approved of by the Governor and Council for the time being, and shall be commissioned and engaged in the same manner that other Military Officers in this Colony are.

ACN

A large wall mounted transcript of the 1741 Charter is on display in the Armory's assembly room providing a proud reminder of the unit's history to all. (See APPENDIX I)

2 d. That the said Company shall have liberty to meet and exercise themselves upon such other days, and as often, as they shall think necessary, and not be subject to orders or directions of the Colonel or other Fieldofficers of the regiment, in whose district they live, in their said meetings and exercisings, and that they be obliged to meet for exercising at least four times in a year; upon the penalty of paying to and for the use of said Company the following fines : viz. the Captain, for each day's neglect, the sum of five pounds, the Lieutenants and Ensign, each forty shillings, the Clerk, the Serjeants, and Corporals, each thirty shillings, and the common soldiers, each twenty shillings, — to be loved by a warrant of distress from the Captain or Superior Officer of said Company for the time being, directed to the Clerk.

3 d. That the said Company, or the greater number of them, shall have power to make such rules and orders amongst themselves as they shall think necessary to promote the end of the establishment, and lay such fines and forfeitures upon any of their own Company, for the breach of any such orders and rules, as they shall think proper, so as the same exceed not forty shillings for any one offence, and also shall have full power to levy the said fines and forfeitures which they shall so impose by a warrant of distress from the Captain or Superior Officer of said Company for the time being, directed to the Clerk.

4th. That all those who shall be duly enlisted in this Company, so long as they continue therein, shall be exempted from bearing arms or doing military duty (watching and warding excepted) in the several Companies or trained bands in whose district they respectively belong, except such as shall at the time be Officers in any of the said Companies.

5th. That the Commission Officers of said Company, from time to time, shall be of the Court Martial and Council of War in the Regiments in whose districts they live.

6th. That if any Officer or Officers of the said Company should be disapproved by the Governor and Council, or should remove out of said town of Newport, or should be taken away by death, — that then, in either of these cases, the Captain of said Company, or the Superior Officer for the time being, shall call the Company together as soon as conveniently may be, and choose others in the room of such Officer or Officers so disapproved, removed, or taken away by death, in the same manner as is hereinbefore directed.

7th. That the Company, at the time of alarm, be under the immediate direction of the Captain-General of the Colony, and that the Officers be commissionated accordingly.

SEALED with the seal of said Colony, by order of the General Assembly.

James Martin, Secretary.

It is noteworthy to observe that the charter is authenticated by the seal of the Colony's General Assembly.

One of the early actions taken by the revived company was to commemorate on February 22, 1794 the anniversary of the birth of the President of the United States, General George Washington. The Company is honored to have received a personal acknowledgment in return from the President.

Chapter **2**

2. The Armory

Due to non-availability of a permanently designated training site, the company assembled and drilled at various places, including the State House, Penrose Hall, Levi Towers Academy, and other convenient venues about town. In 1796, the General Assembly authorized the erection of a gun shed in the rear of the Colony House to provide for the protection of state-owned weaponry in the custody of the artillery company. In due course the drill site was relocated to Clarke Street where Audley Clarke, a member of the company in long standing, on September 16, 1834 sold a lot he owned there, in trust to Stephen Ayrault Robinson, commanding officer of the Artillery Company of Newport, the President of the Town Council and the Attorney General of the State of Rhode Island, for the sum of one dollar.

This set in motion a series of actions that soon resulted in planning and building an armory that would become the company's permanent home after close to 100 years after its initial formation.

Audley Clarke was a merchant in Newport and a member of the Artillery Company for many years. He felt an attachment to the unit, sufficient to prompt him to offer up his lot on Clarke Street so the company could finally build a permanent home and headquarters after being forced to move about town to assemble and drill at diverse sites for many years.

ACN

297 To all People to whom these presents shall come, I Audley Clarke of Newport in the County of Newport in the State of Rhode Island and Providence Plantations, Merchant, Send Greeting. Know ye, That I the said Audley Clarke for and in consideration of my feelings of attachment and good will towards "The Artillery Company of the Town of Newport" a Military Company chartered by the General Assembly of the State of Rhode Island aforesaid, at their February Session Anno Domini 1741. of which Company I have long been a member, and for the purpose of assisting and enabling the said Artillery Company the better to effect the object set forth in their Charter of "acquainting and accustoming themselves to the military exercises by more frequent trainings than the body of the people can attend," and for the further consideration of one dollar to me in hand paid by Stephen Ayrault Robinson, Commanding Officer of said Company, for, and in behalf of said Company, have given, granted, bargained, sold, aliened, enfeoffed, conveyed and confirmed and by these presents do give, grant, bargain, sell, alien, enfeoff, convey and confirm, unto the said Stephen Ayrault Robinson, Commanding Officer of said Company, or his successor in said Office, duly commissioned and engaged, and unto Theophilus Topham, President of the Town Council of the Town of Newport, or his successor in said Office, and unto Albert C. Greene, the Attorney General of the State of Rhode Island aforesaid, or his successor in said Office, One certain lot, or parcel of land, [illegible] Newport aforesaid, butted, bounded and described

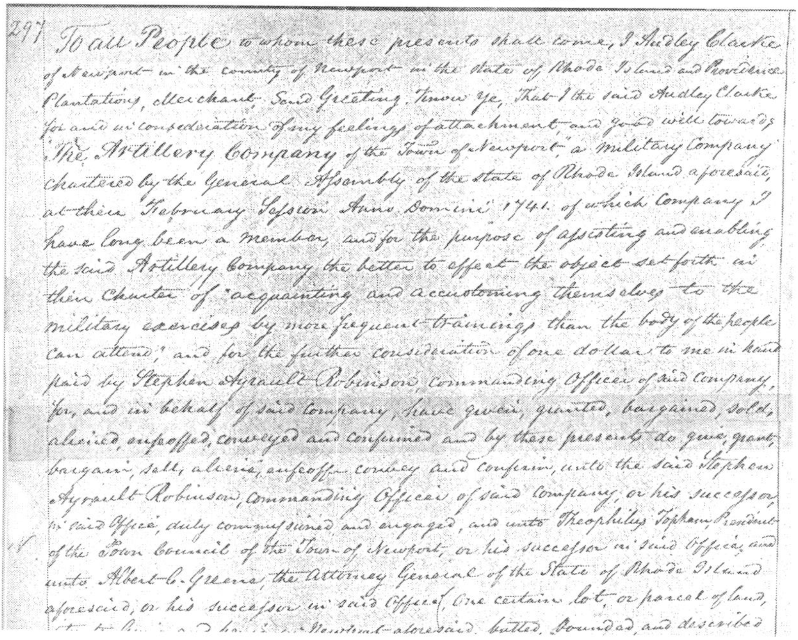

ACN

Shown are two facsimile sections of the deed drawn up on September 16, 1834 and recorded in the Town Clerk's Office of Newport, on November 8th, 1836. Signing for the property were Stephen A. Robinson (of the Artillery Company), Theophilus Topham (President of the Newport Town Council), and Albert C. Greene (Attorney General of the State of Rhode Island).

Clarke and acknowledged the above deed by him signed and sealed to be his voluntary act and deed. Before me

Benj. B. Howland Jus. Peace.

Know all men, That we the said Theophilus Topham, President of the Town Council, Albert C. Greene Att. General and Stephen Ayrault Robinson, Commander of the Artillery Company named in the foregoing deed of Trust accept the premises therein described to be holden on the same conditions as they were held by said Audley Clarke

Stephen A. Robinson
Theophilus Topham

Newport Sept. 16. 1834
Benj. B. Howland witness to S. A. Robinson's signature

William F. Smith witness to signature of Theo. Topham

We hereby accept the foregoing deed in Trust and for the uses and purposes therein mentioned

Albt. C. Greene,
Attorney General.

Witness to signature of Albert C. Greene,
John R. Randolph

Received into my office for recording Newport Nov. 8th 1836 and recorded Nov. 8th 1836. by
Benj. B. Howland Town Clerk

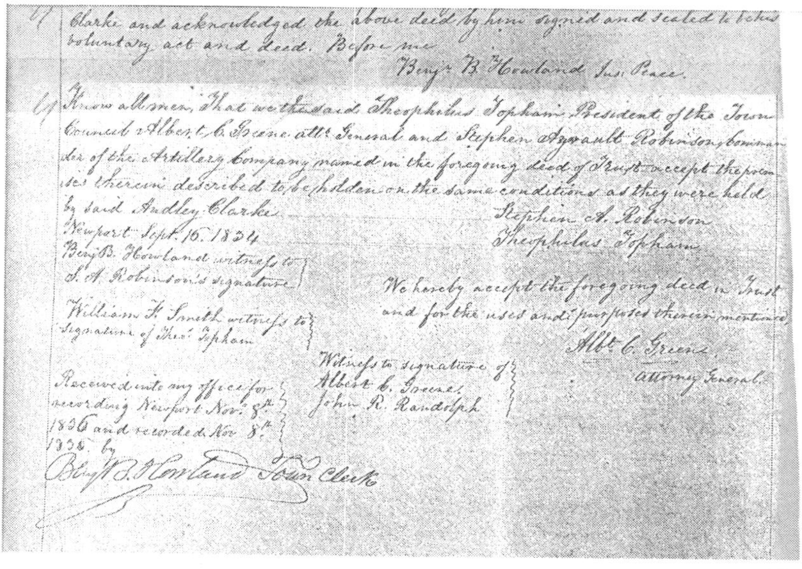

ACN

In the year before being given the land for construction of an armory, the company formed a committee to study the feasibility of such an undertaking. The idea was considered expedient and the General Assembly was petitioned in 1830 for its consent. Thoughts on whether to construct an armory of wood or stone was resolved when Dr. Enoch Hazard offered to make the required stones available for the structure. Potential costs were ascertained and member subscriptions accepted that would support the project. The cornerstone was laid in 1835, but it soon became necessary to curtail certain routine functions to save funds for the building project, including their participation in parades, etc. At one point the walls were built, but funds for the roof were not ascertained. However, a neighbor is said to have come to the rescue and the project went forward to completion. The architect selected was: Joseph M. Darling, and the builder: Keeber and Smith. While the General Assembly did not vote any funds for the construction, it did provide the sum of $700.00 to pay off certain remaining debts in recognition of the company's service during what went down in history as the 'Dorr War', i.e, an armed confrontation prompted by a short-lived insurrection based on the political philosophies among elected leaders and those opposing the rules imposed by the Charter.

ACN

The headquarters of the Artillery Company, America's oldest active military organization, stands on Clarke Street. During the 175 years of its existence, the structure underwent several significant changes. In 1874 the armory was first enlarged to provide more floor space. In the 1880s, a shooting gallery was dug out under the building and a kitchen plus functional rooms were also added. A fire broke out in 1906 destroying portions of the original structure with concurrent loss of valuable artifacts and documents. Reconstruction work included the addition of a second floor with officer's quarters and activity spaces for the troops.

In one of the oldest images of the armory the plain structure of the facility can be readily seen without exterior improvements or any frills. At the time this picture was taken, the men of the Artillery Company posed outside the building, fully uniformed and armed with their assigned muskets. A tree standing near the oversized portal was later removed.

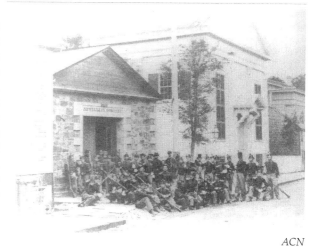

ACN

ACN

In an early bill of accounting for the expenditures of $2,376.21 incurred for the construction of the armory (plus value of the land contributed by Audley Clarke), it is recorded that a 'great deal of work' was contributed gratuitously by the members and others interested in the (Artillery) Corps, with many men working by night and lantern lights in order to complete the project expeditiously. It also notes that the State did not appropriate any funds for the construction of the armory, however a total of $1,900.00 was subsequently made available, including a sum of $300.00 to build a gun house necessary for the protection of field pieces and other equipment belonging to the State.

In 1873, Colonel John Hare Powell, purchased and presented to the Company, one of two paddlewheel cover lunettes that were being removed from the Metropolis, portraying the great eagle and flag, due to conversion of the Fall River Line Steamer from serving as a passenger transport to a railroad car ferry.

The 8′ x 12′ lunette became a popular landmark in Newport and remained mounted on the outside wall above the front entrance to the Armory for many years until it deteriorated so badly that it had to be removed in 1986 because potential falling debris could become a hazard to pedestrians. In seeking a solution to the problem, Mystic Seaport was consulted resulting in agreement by their curator in 1991, to receive and restore the original wooden lunette in exchange for an exact duplicate to be created for the Artillery Company by one of the carvers at Mystic. The replacement carving graces the building in its original beauty.

The popular lunette can be seen here after being originally mounted above the street side entrance to the Armory.

ACN

In this image two cannons assigned to the Artillery Company can be seen in front of the one story Armory building. The large lunette from the passenger liner Metropolis can also be seen above the door.

ACN

BP

At 8:00 a.m. April 27, 1906, a fire was discovered in the Armory that severely damaged a large portion of the roof and badly charred the interior of the one floor structure. Although many artifacts were lost or damaged, Artillery Company members and the fire team identified and saved many items of value. Sgt Thomas Lawton, a long time member of the Company, directed others to places within the Armory where items of value were kept. He personally went into the burning structure repeatedly to save whatever he could.

BP

After the 1906 fire, a Building Committee chaired by Captain Frank King went to work to rebuild the damaged Armory, simultaneously adding a second floor to gain much needed space for the Artillery Company, in particular for the men and their equipment.

ACN

The Commemorative Plaque listing the names of the members of the Building Committee, the Architects and the Contractor, is appropriately displayed as a permanent fixture above the fireplace hearth located in the large upper floor activity room.

DD

The renovated and expanded Armory stands in full glory at the original site, reflecting the outside appearance of the two-story structure, the flag pole and the paddle wheel lunette that had been carried forward from the fire damaged building.

Plaudits must be given to the men charged with mounting and removing the patriotic symbol of Eagle and Flag depicted on what had earlier been an 8′ x 12′ wood carving decorating one of the paddle wheel covers of the passenger ship Metropolis. The installation on the outside of the original one floor armory building took place about 1873. Because of deterioration over the years, it was removed in 1986. In 1991, Mystic Seaport accepted the original carving in exchange for an exact replica that was created by one of their carvers. The replacement carving was then installed on the Armory. Here, the size and weight of the wooden edifice becomes apparent during one of the installations.

ACN

ACN

One cannot imagine the pride of the Artillery Company membership in this September 7, 1913 image, as they mustered in front of their Armory wearing the red-feathered plumes on their hats identifying them as Artillerists, while the historic Eagle and Flag paddle carving from the Metropolis graced the building they called their own. Higher above (outside the frame of the picture) the flag of the United States would have been waving in the wind, making this a most memorable day, both for the soldiers and the onlookers who ventured to Clarke Street to observe the military pageantry.

This view of the Armory on Clarke Street provides an idea of the size of the flagpole that once rose from the sidewalk in front of the building. Next door, is the former meeting house of the Second Congregational Society of Newport that changed hands several times over the years, serving the Central Baptist Society for some time, and was later owned by a Roman Catholic parish. Ultimately the spaces were used for storage purposes. During the Revolutionary War, the building saw use by the military, including the British and the French, at different times.

Of special note is that William Ellery, a signatory of the Declaration of Independence, was a member of the Second Congregational Society, as was William Vernon. Henry Marchant was also a member who assisted in the writing of the Constitution of the United States.

Across the street, about three houses toward the reader, is Vernon House. Built in 1708, this two-story building was once owned by the Collector of Revenue for the British. When the building was sold, it was eventually acquired by William Vernon, son of Newport silversmith Samuel Vernon.

In 1780, French General Rochambeau used Vernon House as his headquarters until his troops departed in 1781. During his stay in Newport he had a number of distinguished visitors, including General George Washington and the Marquis de Lafayette.

DD

BP

The spacious interior offered by the ground level of the expanded and rebuilt armory, was inviting from the beginning. Floor area was plentiful and sufficient for the Company's needs at the time the work was completed. The several artillery pieces in possession of the unit could be attractively displayed when not in use, while at the same time setting aside the space needed to care for, maintain, and train on the cannons to insure their proficient use and handling while in the Company's custody. This helped instill pride in their weaponry and surroundings as the men periodically gathered to clean their powerful entrusted armaments. Wall spaces were soon covered with artifacts and historical paintings of special meaning to this pre-Revolutionary organization.

LFA

BP

Besides gaining much needed billeting spaces on the newly constructed upper floor, the Armory now also provided recreational opportunities for the troops while on duty at this, their Clarke Street home and headquarters. Among these was the pool table shown here, card tables, and skillfully designed seating that ringed the outside walls of the large assembly room to provide storage for the men's personal belongings as well as some of their smaller items of equipment. A well equipped kitchen facility insured the Company was able to feed the troops on site when required.

ACN   *ACN*

There is hardly a time the Company is not ready to show off their treasured artillery pieces, inside the armory, at parades and often in front of the heavy oaken doors of the Armory.

More than a dozen artillery pieces today comprise the array of cannon in possession of the Artillery Company of Newport. Among these are several Civil War pieces, a 75-mm Pack Howitzer, and a restored 6-pound field piece. However, considered the company's most irreplaceable treasure, are four bronze cannons cast at the Paul Revere Foundry near Boston, in 1798.

This likeness of Paul Revere is on display in the Armory. It is placed near the cannon tubes cast at the family foundry.

ACN

ACN

Of special note is the seal of the state of Rhode Island that is affixed to each of the four tubes on display.

ACN

The pride of the Artillery Company. Four original Paul Revere brass cannons are aligned on the parade ground in front of the Naval War College in Newport, where the Company frequently adds to the military pageantry in coordination with naval personnel.

ACN

Fort Adams is from time to time the site chosen by reenactors to not only demonstrate historic drills and battles, but also, to show off their heavy equipment. Here, with tents aligned along the perimeter is their artillery park, where artillery pieces of various calibers are on display.

LFA

Robert Hanley, a longtime member of the Artillery Company, stands proudly beside one of the Paul Revere cannons. Both look polished and ready for inspection by any measure. The statement below, by S.L.A. Marshall summarizes the inner feelings of artillerymen.

Artillerymen have a love for their guns which is perhaps stronger than the feeling of any soldier for his weapon or any part of his equipment.

S. L. A. Marshall

"They Fought to Save Their Guns"

LFA

As they would on any special occasion, the men of the Company assembled at their Armory on July 4th, 1990, readied their equipment, especially the Paul Revere cannons, and then marched to the Colony House to participate in Newport's tribute to America's Independence Day by firing customary salutes to the delight of onlookers who are always on hand at such occasions.

LFA

Author photo

In 1978, on occasion of the 300th Anniversary of the incorporation of the Town of Jamestown (1678) the Artillery Company of Newport rolled out one of its World War I vintage field pieces to display around town as part of the local commemorative exercises.

DD

A Parrot Rifle found its place of honor at the Soldier's Monument in Newport where it can be readily viewed by the public.

Chapter 3

3. The Museum

From the time the Armory was first built, through the years of the fire, its reconstruction and expansion, the facility served the Company's needs very well. The unit was assured adequate space to store and maintain its cannons, muskets, side arms and individual equipment in a secure environment under guard and lock and key.

Following the conclusion of World Wars I and II, some veterans and historians acquired military souvenirs of special interest to them and generally stored and maintained their personal collections in their homes, perhaps to share with good friends and others with similar interests. Fortunately, this group also included several members of the Artillery Company who suggested setting up a museum in the armory for which they would make available their militaria collections for public viewing and appreciation. This was agreed upon in 1960. Initially, items from members' personal collections were displayed. However, it did not take long for other parties to donate items they had brought home from the wars to enhance the collection in the armory. Likewise, the Artillery Company remained alert and ready to ask for uniform donations from military VIPs around the world. Such requests were generally favorably honored.

LFA

Standing outside their armory these men are ready for inspection alongside one of their Paul Revere cannons. Note the Museum sign.

LFA

John Lauth, the Company's first curator (1961), seen here with a rare group of uniforms acquired from the State of Hyderbad after the ruling Nizam was deposed and his private army disbanded in 1947 when the British left India.

LFA

Assistant Curator Elton Manuel showing off his collection of Royal Marine and naval head gear.

LFA

Among the early displays were uniforms tied directly to the history of the Artillery Company of Newport. This side-by-side alignment of uniforms covers the period from approximately 1800 through 1895 as reflected in the head gear worn by the mannequins.

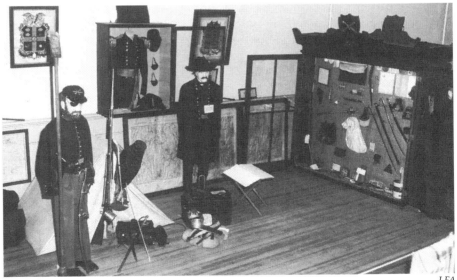

LFA

This area was set aside for a Civil War display, including a tent and personal equipment. Additional time related items appear in the case at the right. The case on the center wall contains an officer's dress uniform with Artillery epaulets.

ACN/TD

The highly treasured Appeal to Heaven flag had its origin in Boston where the Sons of Liberty met at what became known as the Liberty Tree to protest against the taxes imposed by the British Stamp Act of 1765. Ten years later, when the British seized Boston and cut the tree down for firewood, George Washington took that moment to add his now historic words to the image of the tree and developed this meaningful flag.

LFA

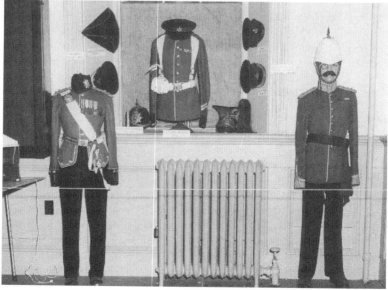

LFA

British, Irish and Scottish uniform attire can be found among the outstanding collection of foreign uniforms on display.

Over the years, students at the Naval War College in Newport have visited the Artillery Company armory and museum routinely as part of their familiarization with the history of Newport and the role it played during the Revolutionary War. Viewing the international displays is of particular interest since they include an array of militaria not found in many repositories of note.

RJ

This group of War College attendees showed a special interest in the Revolutionary War display, and one of the long barreled muskets from that era.

The completely authentic uniform of this British drummer boy attired in a bright red tunic, is remindful of the army of 3,000 redcoats that occupied Newport from 1776 -1779 with another 3,000 Hessians by their side, and the Battle of Rhode Island that was fought in Portsmouth in August 1778.

LFA

ACN/TD

The British Union Jack and superimposed image of Her Majesty Queen Elizabeth II and His Royal Highness The Duke of Edinburgh, tower above the British display of uniforms worn by the finest and most popular and decorated British military leaders of the 20th century.

Author Photo

The Artillery Company is honored to have in its collection the uniform of Fleet Admiral Chester W. Nimitz. He was the commander of the Pacific Fleet following the Japanese attack on Pearl Harbor on December 7, 1941, and directed several campaigns in the Pacific, coordinating with General Douglas MacArthur, who commanded the Southwest Pacific Theater. On September 2, 1945, Fleet Admiral Nimitz accepted the Japanese surrender aboard his flagship, the battleship Missouri.

ACN/TD

We, who survived World War II and were privileged to rejoin our loved ones at home, salute those gallant officers and men of our submarines who lost their lives in that long struggle. We shall never forget that it was our submarines that held the lines against the enemy while our fleets replaced losses and repaired wounds.

C.W. Nimitz, Fleet Admiral, USN.

ACN

General Lyman Lemnitzer served on the Staff of the Allied Force Headquarters in London, under General Dwight D. Eisenhower, and various other responsible positions during and after World War II. In 1963 he rose to the position of supreme Allied Commander of NATO Forces, Europe. Earlier in his military career he served with the 10th Coast Artillery at Fort Adams.

ACN/TD

General Werstmoreland served in various field artillery units before the outbreak of World War II. He saw combat in North Africa and Sicily and took command of the 504th Parachute Infantry Regiment. Later he commanded the Military Assistance Command in Vietnam for a period of time.

ACN/TD

ACN

Colonel Katheine A. Towle, Director of Women Marines from Oct. 18, 1948 thru May 1, 1953. In 1943 she joined a commission in the Women's Reserve of the Marine Corps. She was promoted to Colonel in 1945.

She is seen here at the dedication of an exhibit in her honor at the Artillery Company Museum in October 1972.

LFA

The museum also houses uniform pieces from such great Americans as Army Generals Dwight D. Eisenhower, Mark Clark, Creighton Abrams and Colin Powell.

The items on view are not confined to high ranking military personalities. Displayed are also uniform pieces and related memorabilia from lower ranked personnel, both American and foreign. These include a host of souvenirs and memorabilia dating from the Revolutionary War through the subsequent wars, and on to the present day conflicts in which Americans played a role, including Iraq and Afghanistan.

Not forgotten are World War I, known as the Great War, and World War II which involved many veterans living today, who come to the museum to seek 'their connection' somewhere among the several thousand items available for viewing. Such a journey takes the visitor to the Cold War years when some of America's former World War II allies elected to isolate themselves politically behind what became known as the 'Iron Curtain.'

The Marine Corps tunic worn by LCpl Barton J. Carroll, who was murdered close to home while on furlough in July 2002. His death was unexpected and untimely. He had just completed basic training and was scheduled to attend Munitions School.

ACN/TD

The family of SGT Brinton C. Piez donated his uniform to the Artillery Company in his honor. His Ike-jacket bears the so-called 'Ruptured Duck' patch, worn by many GI's after being discharged from the military service in the early days following the end of World War II, a time when many continued to wear their uniforms while working for the government or pending full integration into civilian life.

DD

ACN/TD

Many small artifacts are displayed in wall sized glass cases to make as many as possible available for public viewing. The majority of items shown here are from World War I.

This group of visitors includes foreign officers and civilian officials attending the Naval War College who are being briefed on the historic armaments that are still in active use at ceremonial exercises of the Artillery Company.

LFA

To acquire and assemble a worthy collection was for the curators a demanding task from the very beginning. Moving beyond their own and other members' personal collections required considerable planning and alertness for the potential availability of rare museum worthy collectibles from a pool of decreasing numbers of popular personalities. Of special interest, of course, were the distinguished military leaders who had endeared themselves to all Americans, thus becoming their heroes and the historic figures for their memorable actions during times of hostility, especially World War II and the Cold War period thereafter.

Personal contacts and networking, combined with an understanding of military courtesy and protocol, plus an affinity of official correspondence, enabled the curators to secure the cooperation of donor sources to obtain some truly one-of-a-kind items that make the Museum of the Artillery Company of Newport unique unto itself and an irreplaceable asset and repository of military memorabilia in the State of Rhode Island.

ACN/TD

The uniform of the late King Hussein of Jordan was donated to the Artillery Company Museum on December 17, 1970. The gift occupies a prominent space among featured world leaders. "He won the respect and admiration of the entire world and so did his beloved Jordan. He is a man who believed that we are all God's children, bound to live together in mutual respect and tolerance." (US President Bill Clinton)

LFA

The Artillery Company is fortunate to have received the only remaining dress uniform of the late Egyptian President Anwar Sadat. He helped overthrow the monarchy in his country in the 1950s and became President in 1970. He earned the Nobel Peace prize in 1978, and was assassinated by Muslim extremists on October 6, 1981.

ACN Web

LFA

An Irish uniform was donated to the museum in 1981. Present for the ceremony, from left to right, were: Curator Elton Manuel, Thomas O'Connor, Mike Kirby, Robert Hanley, and Newport Mayor Robert McKenna.

LFA

Curator Douglas Stamford can be seen here, receiving the donation of another colorful uniform of foreign origin in the presence of J.R. Johnson, Colonel Commanding (1997 - 2000).

LFA

Colonel John Lauth explains Chinese uniforms captured in Korea to a group of Canadian sailors during their visit to the museum in December 1965.

LFA

Foreign officers attending the Naval War College inspect one of the uniforms from the dissolved army of the the Nizam of Hyderbad who was deposed in 1947 when the British left India.

Maintaining the collection of artillery pieces and historic memorabilia in an acceptable condition of preservation and safety is of great concern to the company and the museum's curators, even after the baton of responsibility has been passed on to a replacement after years of service. This necessary effort remains divided among the members of the company, with the gun crews spending time cleaning the cannons, especially after being fired, to insure their safety and operability for the next public appearance. This entails setting up special work times and details to accomplish the tasks at hand, as seen below. Likewise, parts do get worn and may have need to be replaced. Here, a new gun block is being built for the company by students of the woodworking class of Rogers Vocational High School in Newport.

RI

DD

One action that enhanced the prestige and standing of the Artillery Company of Newport is its performance during the short-lived Dorr War, or Dorr Rebellion as it is often referred to, that took place during the May-June period of 1842.

Thomas Wilson Dorr, a lawyer and member of the Rhode Island State legislature (from 1834) organized the 'People's Party' in 1841. He advocated the adoption of a constitution with equal rights regardless of land ownership due to existing imbalanced representation, with the aim of replacing the King Charles Charter of 1663. The legitimate party, i.e. the 'Law and Order Party,' elected Samuel Ward King, Governor, which resulted in an armed confrontation in Providence on May 18,

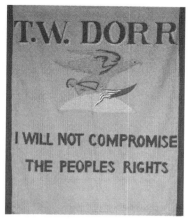

when Dorrites attempted to enter the State House unsuccessfully, then seized two cannons from the United Train of Artillery with plans on attacking the arsenal, which was occupied by 200 men. Governor King called up the Militia, including the Artillery Company of Newport, to put down the uprising, in particular when it appeared the Dorr Party would attempt to employ force by using the cannon in their possession. It appears their gun powder was wet, making it impossible to fire, or, according to another account, they may have lacked the needed gun powder to fire the cannon.

In either case, the Artillery Company of Newport, in part due to being the oldest chartered
ACN/TD artillery company in the state, was given the honor of taking the lead in the State militia's advance on the Dorrite position. On approaching head on, the latter disbanded and moved away toward northern Rhode Island. That concluded the action for the Artillery Company of Newport, earning it the right to operate independently of the Militia's Command, and to take the position on the right flank of the line in perpetuity, which is the most prestigious position in the line of advance.

A second engagement followed several weeks later in Scituate, in which the Artillery Company of Newport once again emerged with plaudits for its soldierly conduct.

Dorr was arrested, tried for treason in 1844, but was released a year later. His actions served to open up the debate on the State's voting and civil rights and related matters that were in due course embraced.

ACN/TD

In this 2013 interior view of the Armory/Museum one can readily recognize many of the items on display from descriptions in earlier chapters. It is fascinating to compare the rudimentary beginnings of the museum in the 1960s when curators John Lauth and Elton Manuel first displayed their personal collections in what were then large and open spaces, to the present time when space is at a premium.

Over the past 50 years the number of items exhibited has multiplied dramatically, particularly as a result of in-kind donations from others, also interested in preserving Rhode Island's military history. This poses ever increasing challenges for the Artillery Company to keep up and maintain in particular, their unique and one-of-a-kind collection of historic military uniforms. Volunteer manpower and financial support are high on the list of the company's needs.

Chapter 4

4. Calls to Duty

Being called to duty can take several forms such as by way of verbal instructions, by being provided written orders either by hand or posting on a bulletin board, or by the firing of a cannon as it happened when the company was called up during the Dorr War. More often however, the Company drummer would beat out a rhythm relaying a message to which the members reacted appropriately by executing a prearranged movement or maneuver. This was particularly appropriate when the unit was assembled or the men within ear's reach. Of course, a drumbeat is always welcomed once a group is assembled, in formation or on the march.

In the 270 plus years since its formation, the drum of the Artillery Company of Newport has been beat thousands of times and the unit called to duty just as often. Sometimes such call would result in providing service at places away from Newport.

Young J. Kurt Lauth beats his drum during a St. Patrick's Day Celebration while another youngster observes with interest the beat and rhythm.

LFA

Once a volunteer was sworn in to serve with the Artillery Company of Newport under the 1741 Charter, obedience to the elected officers and loyalty to the organization became a way of life. This entailed a commitment to report for duty as required, often by way of a written notice. As can be seen from the facsimile announcements appearing here, failure to appear for duty could result in assessment of a fine for absenteeism.

Likewise, the members of the Company were not immune from being brought before a Court Martial board for inappropriate behavior while on duty and wearing the uniform. This prerequisite seems to have been established in a case before a General Court Martial in August 1871, when the charges against an officer were not sustained because he was not on duty when the alleged violation took place, and he was thus considered a volunteer civilian who could not be tried by a military court.

PROCEEDINGS

OF A

GENERAL COURT-MARTIAL,

HOLDEN AT NEWPORT, AUGUST 1, 1817,

FOR THE TRIAL OF

CAPTAIN ROBERT B. CRANSTON,

OF THE

NEWPORT ARTILLERY,

AS OFFICIALLY REPORTED BY THE

JUDGE ADVOCATE.

Copy Right Secured.

The Defence of the prisoner consisted of two parts :
1st. To the Jurisdiction : 2d. To the Merits.

And the Court-room being cleared of all persons except the Court and Judge Advocate, after mature deliberation, the following question was put to each member of the Court, beginning with the member lowest in grade, viz. " Shall the jurisdiction of this Court as to the first charge be sustained, or not ;" and the Court were of opinion, that the jurisdiction thereof be not sustained.

The Court adjourned until to-morrow morning, at 8 o'clock.

WEDNESDAY MORNING, *August* 6, 1817.

Present.—All the Court, the Judge Advocate and Marshal. And the Court-room being cleared of all persons except the Court and Judge Advocate, after mature deliberation, the following question was put to each member, beginning with the lowest in grade, viz. " Shall the jurisdiction of this Court as to the second charge be sustained, or not ;" and the Court were of opinion, that the jurisdiction thereof be not sustained. Court adjourned *sine die.*   ALBERT C. GREENE,

Brig. Gen. 4th Brigade, PRESIDENT.

HENRY BOWEN, JUDGE ADVOCATE.

In 1757, eleven members of the Artillery Company, chosen by lot, joined the British in the French-Indian War, serving at Crown Point and at Fort William Henry in upper New York. All returned home safely.

Loyalties changed during the Revolutionary War when some of the members left Newport to join the colonists. Others stayed behind and sided with the British until their departure in 1779.

The war of 1812 found the Artillery Company in a high state of readiness. Some of the men were assigned to augment forces on Goat Island and the North Battery. Roving patrols were formed to roam the beaches. In 1813 Oliver Hazard Perry readied an expedition to Put-in-Bay on Lake Erie for which men of the company were detached so they could join him on his venture. Altogether, the Rhode Island contingent accounted for 236 persons that followed him. After a highly successful deployment away from home, the group returned, however many were ill from gastroenteritis, while others suffered from typhoid fever. In total, six deaths were reported.

Commodore Oliver Hazard Perry

Flagship Niagara in Process of Restoration

Perry's flag was given to the Artillery Company twenty years after the battle of Lake Erie. The slogan "We have met the enemy and they are ours" is attributed to him. The above image shows the Perry display at the museum. His body was returned to Newport in 1826.

ACN/TD

RE

Inauguration of Governor Bruce Sundlun on January 1st, 1991. The Artillery Company joined the 103rd Field Artillery "Guards of Thunder" in rendering honors for the new Governor.

On April 16, 1861, the Artillery Company of Newport was hastily notified to assemble at the armory. The men were advised that President Lincoln had issued a call for 75,000 men. Everyone volunteered and the unit became Company "F" (color company) of the 1st Rhode Island Detached Militia. Thirteen men remained at the Armory in Newport while the main body proceeded to Washington for three months. While there, they were quartered in the Patent Office until Camp Sprague was ready to receive them. They paraded to the White House repeatedly and were reviewed by the President several times. In July, the unit fought at the First Bull Run covering the Union retreat after the battle. Although mustered out upon their return home, many enlisted in other units being formed in the State only to fight again. Those remaining at the armory became instructors for others.

In 1862, Lovell Hospital operated at Portsmouth Grove (Melville) where, for three years, some 1,700 sick and wounded Union and Confederate soldiers were treated. In July, some 20 to 50 men from the Artillery Company performed guard duty at this Civil War facility. This service was repeated from time to time.

At the outbreak of the Civil War, Ambrose Burnside was a Brigadier General in the Rhode Island Militia. He raised a regiment, the 1st Rhode Island Volunteer Infantry, and was appointed its Colonel on May 2, 1861. Two companies were armed with Burnside Carbines. He soon became Brigade Commander and commanded the brigade at the First Bull Run.

RE

The Rhode Island Memorial at New Bern Cemetery in North Carolina where Company "F" fought alongside General Burnside's troops.

ACN Web

Two gun crews perform a drill before the public on February 22, 1890, apparently as part of that day's exercises celebrating George Washington's birthday.

ACN

During the Spanish-American War (1898), the company provided a detail of personnel to guard Fort Adams while the regulars were away on assignments elsewhere. Ordnance Sergeant Thomas H. Lawton (center front) was among the group on temporary duty at the fort.

In September 1860 an earlier detail of 4 officers, 24 men and 2 musicians were temporarily stationed at Fort Adams since the federal government had phased down the facility due to shortage of funds.

ACN/TD

At this drill in the late 1800s, fife and drummers posed to show off their instruments. Although the Artillery Company of Newport fielded a small musical unit on several occasions over the years, this group of artillery men seem to represent a number of different commands.

RE

A montage displaying the images of the Artillery Company's officers serving on the staff of Colonel Frank P. King, Commanding. The Colonel headed the company from 1909 to 1914.

RE

Members of the Artillery Company in dress uniforms and headgear of 1890 vintage, and below, a group of officers with uniforms representative of the Civil War period.

RE

The standard of the Artillery Company of Newport was designed by Rev. Dom. Wilfred Bayne, a monk at the Portsmouth Priory. He designed the flag after interpreting an old description of the original Company flag. The standard is two-sided, with one side showing the Rhode Island Colonial seal (anchor with rope) and the other, the coat of arms of Rhode Island's Governor Wanton. The national ensign of Great Britain is located in the upper corners of both sides. The flag is a duplicate of the original 1775 issue and was presented to the Company by the United Veterans Council at a ceremony at Battery Park in mid-August, 1965.

ACN/TD

"The Newport Artillery in battle," as depicted in a painting by Alfred Richardson Simson. He presented the painting at the 250th Anniversary of the company in August 1991.

LFA

At an Army Day celebration, often held at Fort Adams, Arthur F. Newell, Colonel Commanding from 1976 to 1978, can be seen standing in front of a line of artillery pieces displayed by the Artillery Company of Newport. Examples of the heavy weaponry used in the wars since the unit was chartered in 1741 were on hand for viewing.

ACN

The entire unit turned out for this group photograph taken in front of the Armory sometime in the 1930s. The uniform changed only slightly during the period between World War I and World War II, except that open collars were permitted.

Throughout the years of its existence, the Artillery Company has emphasized the need for small arms proficiency of its members. Thus, there is hardly a time in the past when the Company was not at work preparing a qualified rifle team to pit against similar teams from among other Militia units in the area.

RE

During the period 1904 - 1905 this Artillery Company Rifle Team held the title of State Champions by winning 6 out of 6 matches in competition and beating the next highest score with 1481 versus 1373 points. Although the team consisted of artillery men, its members were selected for their individual marksmanship skills.

RE

This earlier team is assembled outside the Armory about 1895, always ready for a 'good shoot'.

RE

In 1918, motorized transport to the Rumford Rifle Range was arranged for these 20 men.

Another detail awaits orders to proceed from the Armory on Clarke Street in Newport to the Rumford Firing Range for rifle practice.

DD

Artillery Company members pose in civilian attire following their 1971 musket shoot in which the marksmen annually prove their accuracy in firing aging muskets. From left to right: COL John Lauth, holding the cherished Gibbs Championship trophy, SGT David Dewhurst, CAPT Robert Hanley, LT Bernard Northrup, Major Fred Kirby, LT Neil Huntley, and CAPT James Brady.

In 2010, the Artillery Company's Musket Team took first place in a shooting competition among all Rhode Island's militia units. Each team of five fired five rounds per man using flint lock muskets at a range of 25 yards. Colonel Roy Lauth of the Artillery Company won the Commander's Award, scoring 48 out of 50 points. He also received the Gibbs Medal for his high score among the Company's shooters. Participants from left to right: CPL Craig Mulvey, COL Roy Lauth, LTC Michael Pine, XO, PVT John A. Connor, CAPT Kenneth L. Pike, COL Robert Edenbach, Colonel Commanding.

ACN Web

ACN Web

Both in 1989 and 1990, the Artillery Company of Newport won the cannon competition trophy from among the participating militia units of the State of Rhode Island. In both years the competitions were held at Camp Fogarty.

LFA

Fatigues are worn for field work and practice firing, however, for the reenactment of a special event, dress uniforms are the order of the day.

HEADQUARTERS NEWPORT ARTILLERY.

CHARTER GRANTED 1741

NEWPORT ARTILLERY Co

FIAT JUSTITIA RUAT COELUM

City of Newport, Nov 26 1912

This is to Certify

That George Rodda

has this day been duly elected a member of this Company, agreeably to its Charter and By-Laws

James W Thompson, Clerk & Qr. Mr.

Frank P. King, Colonel Commanding.

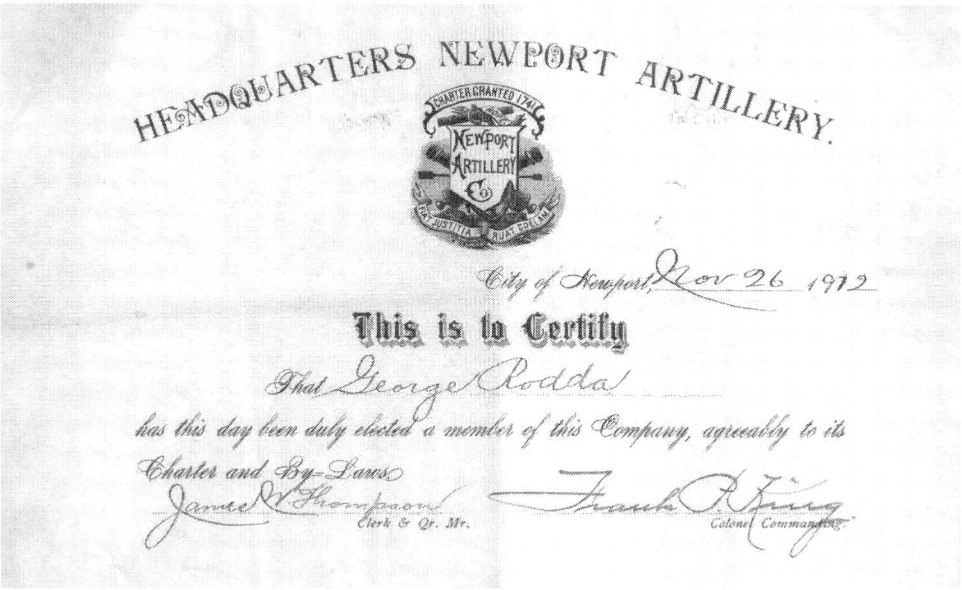

ACN

The two documents shown here are unique and of special interest in that they represent the election of George Rodda to membership in the Artillery Company in 1912, followed by his discharge from service of the State in 1917, to permit him to enter the National Army (World War I).

Rhode Island Militia.

To all whom it may Concern:

Know Ye, That George W. F. Rodda.

a Sergeant of Captain Newport Artillery Co

Company of the of the

Rhode Island Militia,

who was mustered in on the twenty-sixth day of November

one thousand nine hundred and twelve to serve 3 year

is hereby **Discharged** from the service of the State, this fourth day of October

1917, at Newport R.I. by reason of entering the National Army

Service honest and faithful

(No objection to his being re-enlisted is known to exist.)*

A. K. Barker.

Commanding.

*This sentence will be erased if there is anything in the conduct or physical condition of the soldier rendering him unfit for the Militia.

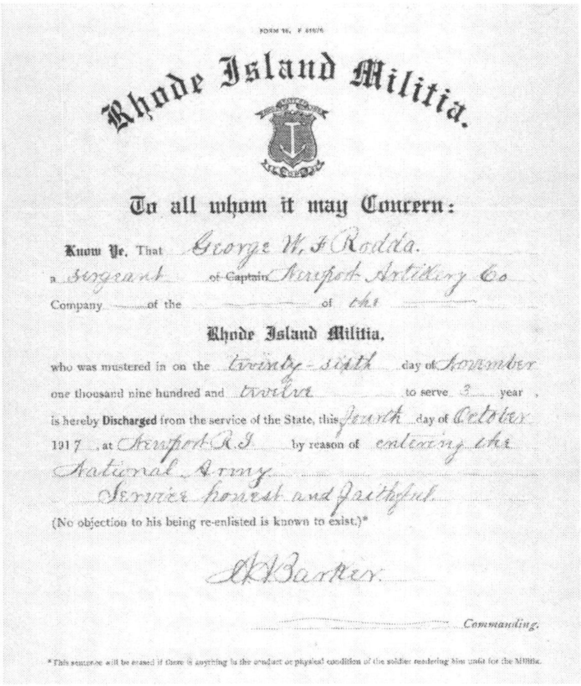

ACN

ACN/TD

Newport Artillery Company member SGT Paul Cairrao, while serving in Iraq with the 103rd Field Artillery of the Rhode Island National Guard, proudly displayed the guidon of the Artillery Company during his tour of duty from 2004 - 2005.

RE

JD

In 1992, a company member, while on active duty with the Rhode Island National Guard, mounted a Newport Artillery Company guidon on his humvee as he entered Kuwait City along with other American troops. In 2004, during Operation Iraqi Freedom, the guidon was once again flown where the action was. Shown here, is a guidon that has been specially embroidered to commemorate the time it was displayed in the overseas war zone.

Company member John Duchesneau served several tours overseas with the Rhode Island National Guard. His assignments in 2003-04 and 2005-06 took him to Iraq, Afghanistan and Guantanamo Bay.

Chapter 5

5. Historical Functions

Whether in the early years while operating as an organized Militia unit, or in present times when the Newport Artillery Company's responsibilities have evolved to being that of a celebrated ceremonial unit of the Council of Historic Military Commands, in the State of Rhode Island, the members of the organization have for the past 270 plus years paraded on the streets of many area municipalities, bound by their commitment to the original Charter of 1741, as subsequently modified, without regard to their changed organizational status. Thus, the following photographs allow the reader to experience the various marching formations over a period of many years. One need only compare the uniforms among the several images to appreciate the passage of time. Today, the Company provides cannon salutes, color guards, and honor guards for official state and local ceremonies, as well as for privately sponsored patriotic and veterans' events.

TD

COL John L.R. Macomber, RIM, MAJOR GEN Reginald Centracchio, Adjutant General State of Rhode Island, BRIGADIER GEN Richard Valente, Officer in Charge of the historical commands of RI, shown here congratulating COL Macomber on his assuming command of the Artillery Company of Newport on May 12, 1996.

Over the years, the Artillery Company has marched the parade routes on foot as others had done before. Whenever artillery pieces were included in the procession, horses were required to help move the heavy loads, making them an integral part of the formation. Following World War I, the first motorized tractors and transports became available for occasional use, signs of changes on the horizon. These changes would, over time, not only affect equipment and weaponry, but uniforms and organizational arrangements as well.

ACN   *ACN*

The Artillery Company on the march in the late 1880s. The units 'on foot' and with horse drawn Civil War field pieces appear to be proceeding along Bellevue Avenue.

LFA

The Artillery Company on a training exercise near Two Mile Corner, about 1900.

RE

At a parade in the 1920s, this unique and seldom seen motorized weapons tractor and transport received much attention from the onlookers.

The members of the Newport Artillery Company are known to favor marching to their own drum beat, maintaining their organizational independence under which they have operated for over 270 years.

Author Photo

Enroute to a change of Command Ceremony to be held in front of the Colony House in Newport.

ACN

To participate in the Victory Parade for the 1st Iraq War the Company turned out with fife and drum to pace the procession of members clad in the uniforms of past wars.

Specially tailored quasi 1812 uniforms became the company's standard ceremonial dress for a period about the time of commemorative exercises honoring Admiral Perry at Put-in-Bay in 1913. Additional images show Company members wearing these special uniforms at various other occasions.

RE

RE

RE

LFA

Company members dressed in uniforms styled to resemble the War of 1812 era. This group assembled at the Raytheon facility in Portsmouth, RI on October 19, 1965.

LFA

Governor J. Joseph Garrahy marches with Colonel Adrian Surette at his side during a May 14 Rhode Island Independence Day celebration.

DD

A 1990 rendering of the Old Colony House by artist Marjorie Vogel. Newport's Colony House is the 4th oldest State House still standing in the United States.

TD

LFA

Major Jim Brady leads column of Artillery Company marchers at the National Police Parade on Bellevue Avenue in the 1970s.

On October 24, 2001, a historic flag raising took place at Fort Adams in Newport. Throngs of people turned out to witness the ceremony. The March of the Colors was led by members of the Artillery Company wearing the uniforms of the many engagements the unit had participated in, from the time of its formation in 1741, through to the modern day wars. The oversized flag was raised on the fort's new pole during the thunder of a memorable 21-gun salute.

Author Photo

LFA

Members of the Artillery Company muster in front of their armory on Clarke Street dressed in World War I uniforms, ready to participate in an Armistice Day celebration.

ACN

In 1790, the Artillery Company served as a body guard for President George Washington during his visit to Newport. To this date, the Company can be depended on to muster an Honor Guard at the local General Washington monument in celebration of the President's birthday. From left: Roy Lauth, Andrew Jones, LTC Mike Pine, Brandon Aglio, and Leslie Pine.

LFA

Here, honors were extended to President George Washington at the statue outside the Redwood Library. From left: Chris Gagliarti, Charles M. "Matt" Dick, Jack Goode, unidentified, and Colonel John Macomber.

RE

COL Fred Kirby (seated), is honored by family and friends at the armory in 2000 after being awarded the Rhode Island Star by MGEN Reginald Centracchio, RI Adjutant General.

RE

The Newport Artillery Company turned out in force for the 2006 Memorial Day exercises at City Hall. Among the participants were veterans of World Wars II, Korea and Vietnam. Standing from left to right are: Geoffrey Gardener, Kaylee Pike, Mike Pike, Fred Kirby, Doug Stamford, Frank Hale, John Drotes, Jack Goode, Henry Fletcher, Harry Warner, Robert Edenbach, and Roy Lauth.

RE

At the Gettysburg Gun ceremony on the State House Lawn in Providence, on July 3, 2013, LTC Mike Pine and 2LT Leslie Coutu joined in the activities wearing uniform and dress of the Civil War period.

RE

Artillery Company members (from left) Frank Hale, Robert Edenbach and Robert Goode, wearing World War II uniforms, participate in the August 12, 2013, VJ Day exercises.

ACN

4th of July celebration near the old Army-Navy building in Newport.

ACN

Aligned to celebrate the Bicentennial in 1976 while salutes are fired, are from left: Major Jim Brady, Colonel Harold E. "Zeke" St. John and Colonel Fred Kirby.

Author Photo

Official Change of Command ceremonies are often held at Fort Adams, a site to which the Artillery Company is historically connected. As a member of the Historical Commands of Rhode Island the official transfer of the company's leadership authority is witnessed by Brigadier General Richard Valente, representing the Rhode Island National Guard.

LFA

Artillery Company members take on the role of Colonial Marines during a drill aboard the replica Sloop Providence in October 1977.

Author Photo

Member Dan Titus at Fort Adams during the first Civil War weekend in the early 2000s. He is standing next to a bronze Model M-1841 6-pound cannon manufactured at the Ames foundary in Chicopee, Massachusetts in 1845.

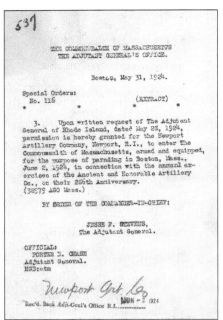

ACN

Protocol and 'the Rules' must be followed before moving the company "armed and equipped" across State lines as can be seen in this 1924 letter from the Adjutant General's Office of the Commonwealth of Massachusetts.

ACN

On September 11, 2009, the Artillery Company participated in the making of a commercial for the N.E. Patriots, entitled: The Patriot. Filming took place at the Boston Common. In this instance, the Company was prevented from using black powder during their reenactment scene. Colonel Robert Edenbach can be seen here consulting with David Loda, the Paul Revere reenactor for that event.

SF

Company members turn out to honor Governor William Ellery at his resting place in the Common Burial Ground of Newport each 4th of July. Ellery is among the signatories of the Declaration of Independence. The men firing the salute are, from left: Tom Donnelly, Scott Reese, Brandon Aglio and Mike Pine, XO.

SF

LFA

Two bronze AMES Model M-1841 6-pound field guns take their place of honor at the Civil War burial site in Island Cemetery, Newport. One of the guns seen here was destroyed by a falling tree limb during a hurricane in the sixties. The barrel and metal parts were recovered and put in storage. In 1972 the carriage was rebuilt by students at Rogers High School, under the guidance of Clyde Allen, the school's wood shop instructor. It was later returned to service with the Artillery Company of Newport.

Susan Pieroth

An AMES gun on Clarke Street in 1891. Attending the weapon, from left to right are: James P. Wetherill, Louis R. Mumford, George S. Flagg, Thomas S. Tilley, Corporal M.W. Wetherill, John O. Brightman, Sergeant C.T. Bliss, and Charles A. Palmer.

Chapter **6**

6. Honors, Social Functions and Encampments

The Artillery Company of Newport has served honorably in all the military actions and campaigns in which it participated as far back as 1757 when it served with the British in the French Indian War. Although a militia unit, the company has been honored repeatedly for its dedicated performance when most needed. The company has been awarded a special battle streamer for each campaign in which it participated to display on their flag as a sign of the special honors bestowed upon the unit, much as is practice among the federal military.

LFA

On January 16, 1970, Lieutenant Governor Joseph J. Garrahy of Rhode Island, signed a bill for the Artillery Company streamers. In attendance from left: Major Frederick Kirby, RIM, CPT James J. Brady, RIM, MAJ Elton M. Manuel, RIM, LT Gov. Garrahy, Colonel John P. Lauth, RIM, and Senator Erich A. O'D Taylor.

At a special Streamer Pageant in 2003, Colonel John Lauth pins an awarded streamer on the Artillery Company flag. At this occasion he wore the same style uniform he wore as a Corporal in World War II while a member of the 28th Division, 112th Infantry.

During above program the invited guests witnessed local military pageantry few had ever experienced. Individual streamers were presented to the tune of military music from the respective streamer's war or campaign. The evolution of the marching tunes alone, told the story of the historical changes the Company has experienced during the 250 plus years of its existence.

Time	War/Campaign	Prevailing Tune
1741 -	Charter Year	God Save the Queen
1755 -	French and Indian War	Rule Brittania
1775 - 1781	Revolutionary War	Yankee Doodle
1812 -	War of 1812	Hail, Columbia
1842 -	Dorr Rebellion	Green Grow the Rushes
1861 - 1865	Civil War	Battle Hymn of the Republic
1898 -	Spanish American War	Hot Time in the Old Town Tonight
1917 - 1918	World War I	Over There

Saint Barbara is the patron Saint of artillery men worldwide. She is also the patron of armorers, gunsmiths, miners, and others exposed to gunpowder and explosives. Her powers are invoked against thunder and lightning. Annually, on December 4th, Saint Barbara's Day, the Artillery Company of Newport hosts a special celebration in her honor at which the Legend of Saint Barbara is read to those assembled at the Armory during these traditional exercises.

The legend has it that Barbara was born in the Middle East around the third century. She was imprisoned in a tower by her pagan father, who jealously feared that she would marry. Saint Barbara requested three windows be installed in the tower of her captivity, symbolizing the Trinity of her recently adopted Christianity. When her father learned that she had adopted the new faith, he killed her and was himself immediately struck dead by a lightning bolt.

ACN

In 1996, the U.S. Field Artillery Association bestowed the Ancient Order of St. Barbara upon the Artillery Company of Newport. This honor enables the Company to bestow the Honorable Order of Saint Barbara upon others who meet the awards criteria.

RJ

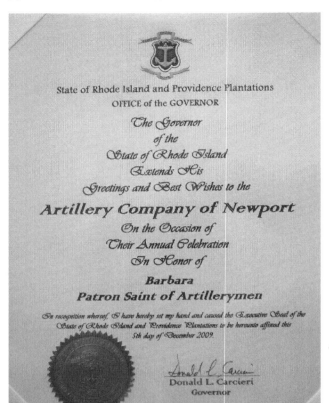

State of Rhode Island and Providence Plantations
OFFICE of the GOVERNOR

The Governor
of the
State of Rhode Island
Extends His
Greetings and Best Wishes to the

Artillery Company of Newport

On the Occasion of
Their Annual Celebration
In Honor of

Barbara
Patron Saint of Artillerymen

In recognition whereof, I have hereby set my hand and caused the Executive Seal of the State of Rhode Island and Providence Plantations to be hereunto affixed this 5th day of December 2009.

Donald L. Carcieri
Governor

Annually, the Governor of the State of Rhode Island extends his best wishes to the Artillery Company on occasion of their annual celebration in honor of Saint Barbara, Patron Saint of Artillerymen.

ACN/TD

As might be expected, a small statue of the Patron Saint Barbara is among the cherished artifacts held in the Museum collection of the Artillery Company of Newport.

RJ

During the 1989 Saint Barbara celebration, LTCOL E.M. Manuel, RIM, is awarded the Long Service (7 years) Militia Badge from MGEN Leonard Holland, Adjutant General of Rhode Island.

LFA

LFA

On occasion of the U.S. Army's birthday in 1971, a sterling silver punch bowl was presented to the Artillery Company of Newport, "in Admiration and Affection from past and present U.S. Army Officers at the Naval War College." The Army's senior advisor at the War College had collected sterling silver military insignia from previous and present U.S. Army students that were melted down and from which the punch bowl was later designed. Army Colonel John Keely presented the bowl to Colonel John Lauth of the Artillery Company.

ACN

Colonel Robert Edenbach is assisted by Major Geoffrey Gardner during enlistment exercises for Chelsey Coleman.

ACN

Robert Edenbach, Colonel Commanding, presents the Commanding Officer's Award to Captain Joanne Pike, Adjutant, for her dedicated service over a long time.

The following copy is an award executed by Governor John Collins in 1786, representing the election and designation of John Malbone as Brigadier General of the Militia in the County of Newport. John Malbone was in command of the Artillery Company for 17 years, from 1775 to 1792. Although the company experienced a long period of inactivity during and immediately following the Revolutionary War, Malbone was instrumental in seeking and obtaining the consent of the Rhode Island General Assembly, in 1792, to revitalize to company under its original charter.

ACN

1981 Governor's designation of John P. Lauth, as Lieutenant in the Rhode Island Militia (Naval Battalion).

ACN

LFA

In 1971, the Artillery Company celebrated its 240th Anniversary. Elton Manuel, did the honors of cutting the cake. With him, from left to right, are: Corporal Mark Coleman, John P. Lauth, Colonel Commanding, and J. Coleman.

LFA

Well wishes are exchanged between Colonel Roy Lauth (right), and a reenactor of George Washington, at a reenactment of the arrival of the President in Newport.

An 1855 Invitation to the "Sixth Annual Ball" at the Bellevue Hall in Newport.

Formal dances require a knowledge of the social graces that were expected of the officers and their spouses in years past.

LFA

Awaiting guests at a formal dinner in September 1965. Colonel Lauth keeps a watchful eye on etiquette and behavior.

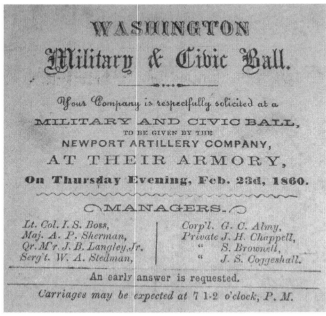

LFA

This Invitation is for a Military and Civic Ball to be held at the Armory on Clarke Street on occasion of George Washington's birthday.

The Artillery Company of Newport is Rhode Island's leading Militia Unit based on its historical standing, having gained certain privileges and honors during the Dorr War and other engagements. Always aware of its meager beginnings, the company must pay continuing attention to its performance as a quasi military entity while simultaneously meeting social expectations of the past and present. To accomplish these goals requires dedication, loyalty and hard work. To gain a better understanding of life and habits in the 1800s, the company periodically engages in reenactments away from the pleasantries of home, without broadcasting that it can all be broadly categorized as "training," an element always present.

ACN Web

Major Robert Edenbach and Major Palmer Hedly cast round musket balls for their 75 caliber smoothbore muskets.

ACN Web

In Battery F, everyone shares in the chores while in the field. Here, the washing of dishes is accompanied by shoptalk.

ACN Web

Camping out in a semi military setting does have its relaxing moments. Here, Captain Joanne Pike and other members of Battery F enjoy a few laughs under the fly of the Sanitary Commission tent.

ACN Web

At day's end, there is time to relax throughout the camping area, and members can enjoy the off-duty hours at the Sanitary Commission tent, with family members present.

7. Personages

All the men and women who ever served the Artillery Company of Newport in what ever capacity, are worthy of special plaudits. Taking into account the deeds and accomplishments of the many dedicated members, the service of one individual, i.e. Sergeant Thomas Lawton, stands out as a beacon of light among all who have served before and after him because of the many years of his life he gave to the benefit of the Company. In an 1889 publication, his service was described as follows:

"Among the non-commissioned officers none is more worthy of special mention than Sergeant of Ordinance Thomas H. Lawton, who has held that position since February, 1876, and to whose care the excellent condition of the guns and accoutrements of the company give the highest recommendation."

Ordnance Sergeant Thomas H. Lawton, born in Newport in 1835, joined the Artillery Company of Newport in April 1860. He was a member of the unit when it was activated as Company F, 1st Rhode Island Detached Militia, in 1861. He is one of a few that saw active military service in the Civil War, Spanish-American War and the First World War. Lawton died in 1923 after having served an astonishing 63 years as a member of Newport's honored Artillery Company.

ACN TD

Following are recent-time images of Artillery Company members elected to the leadership position of Colonel-Commanding for the respective period shown:

ACN/TD

COL Robert S.
Edenbach,
63rd Commander,
2008 - Present

ACN/TD

COL Geoffrey D. Gardner,
62nd Commander,
2004-2008

ACN/TD

COL Roy D. Lauth,
61st Commander,
2000-2004

ACN/TD

COL James R. Johnson,
60th Commander,
1997-2000

ACN/TD

COL John L.R, Macomber,
59th Commander,
1996-1997

ACN/TD

COL Frank S. Hale,
58th Commander,
1992-1996

ACN/TD

COL John P. Lauth,
50th Commander,
1969-1973

Senior staff members of the Company visited their old comrade and friend, Frederick Kirby at his home in February 2008 to congratulate him on being elevated to the rank of Brigadier General (BG) in the Rhode Island Militia. At an official ceremony at the armory, Major General Robert Bray, Adjutant General for the State of Rhode Island, presented the General's credentials. In 2000, BG Kirby had been awarded the Rhode Island Star by Major General Centracchio, then Rhode Island's Adjutant General. BG Kirby was the 52nd Colonel Commanding of the Artillery Company from 1973-1976, and a member for forty-six years. He died in 2011 at age 97.

ACN

The Staff members visiting BG Kirby (from left) are: COL Frank Hale, COL Robert Edenbach, the Rev. LTC Everett Greene, the son Alan Kirby, and LTC Mike Pine.

In his capacity of Captain-General and Commander-in-Chief (of the Rhode Island Militia), Governor John H. Chafee, on September 24, 1963, ordered the Artillery Company to provide a military escort for General Dwight D. Eisenhower on his arrival in Newport on September 26th. At that time, General Eisenhower had been retired from the office of President of the United States for six years.

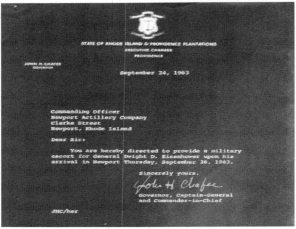

ACN

General Eisenhower visited Newport several times from January 1953 to January 1961 while holding the office of the 34th President of the United States. Here, he can be seen in 1963, speaking with COL Harold E. "Zeke" St. John of his Artillery Company military escort at the dedication of Eisenhower Park on Washington Square in Newport.

ACN

ACN

The Artillery Company of Newport was called out on July 10, 1976, to provide an honor guard for Britain's Queen Elizabeth II during her Bicentennial visit to the United States. Newport's Mayor Humphrey Donnelly III, and his wife Barbara greeted the Queen and her husband Prince Phillip of Edinburgh at Trinity Church where she unveiled a plaque dedicating Queen Anne Square. A formal dinner aboard the Queen's Yacht Britannia followed, with President Ford and members of his Cabinet in attendance.

Her Royal Highness Princess Margaret, Countess of Snowdon, visited Newport on July 16, 1988, to participate in a fund raiser for the Preservation Society of Newport. During a formal dinner sponsored by the Newport Press Society at the Breakers, the Princess, as guest of honor, was presented a Swarovski crystal pineapple on behalf of the Preservation Society by COL John Lauth of the Artillery Company.

LFA/Corbett

LFA

MGEN William Westmoreland attending a ball at Belcourt Castle on occasion of the 250th Anniversary of the Artillery Company of Newport. Among the dignitaries attending were (front row from left): COL Harold E. "Zeke" St. John, R.I. Governor John Notte, and Admiral and Mrs. Weschler. The event was arranged by the Newport Preservation Society.

RJ

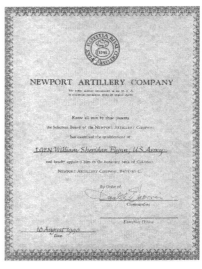

ACN

A Newporter by birth, LTGEN William Sheridan Flynn, U.S. Army (Ret.), visited the Museum in August 2013 in the company of his brother, Navy CDR John J. Flynn. He is seen here with curator Ron Jones of the Artillery Museum. General Flynn was appointed honorary Colonel of Battery 'C, in 1990. Before his retirement in 1992 he had been Chief of Staff of the Army Materiel Command, and later, head of the U.S. Army Tank-Automotive Command (TASCOM).

Robert Edenbach, Colonel Commanding of the Artillery Company, representing Rhode Island's oldest military organization, speaks with MGEN Robert Bray, RI Adjutant General, in 2008, then head of Rhode Island's modern day National Guard component.

RE

RE

MGEN Robert Bray, Adjutant General of the State of Rhode Island, officiates at the 2008 Change-of-Command ceremony of Robert Edenbach, who had been elected Colonel Commanding of the Artillery Company of Newport.

The Artillery Company Museum is open to the public on published dates, as well as by special appointment. Groups with given historical interests can also be accommodated with advance notice. Following is a cross section of groups that have visited the museum in recent times.

RJ

Mike Pine, Executive Officer of the Artillery Company, takes his turn in briefing a visiting group from American Legion Post #18, in May 2012.

RJ

Students of the Naval War College often visit the exhibits at the Artillery Company Museum. On such an occasion in June 2012, Mike Pine, XO of the Artillery Company is on hand to explain the various types of cannon on display.

TD

SGT Ron Jones, Curator at the Artillery Museum, explains the use of the great chain that was once floated across the Hudson River to protect West Point from the British. Viewing the exhibit are, from left to right: URI ROTC Cadet Bryan Shapow, URI ROTC Cadet Michael Garrity, and CAPT Ansalem T.W. Richards, U.S. Army Assistant Professor of Military Science at URI.

RJ

Veterans of the 3rd Marine Division and their wives give the appearance of being satisfied after viewing the exhibits and holding an organizational meeting in the conference area above the museum. Groups such as these perpetuate interest in the unique displays the Artillery Company of Newport can offer for public appreciation.

Castellano Photo

A visit to the Artillery Museum in June 2013, turned out to be a fun day for Serena Cucco who was visiting Newport with her father and Carol Castellano, Director of Programs of the National Organization of Parents of Blind Children. Serena enjoyed the opportunity of learning that Prince Phillip of Britain had donated the jacket of his Royal Navy uniform to the museum, and that he had worn it aboard HMS Whelp as a Lieutenant when Japan surrendered in Tokyo Bay, ending World War II in 1945.

Serena made the best of it for the day by examining various military artifacts of interest. She was fascinated at the variety of 'touchable' display items on hand that helped to explain their origin and purpose. This jeep, helmets and cannon balls received a full inspection by this truly interested visitor.

Castellano Photo

The author, Walter Schroder (left), and his German classmate Eberhard Leithold, enjoyed their visit to the museum in 1997. Of particular interest was the uniform of Field Marshal Montgomery of Alamein. They had both been drafted from High School in Germany at age 15 and assigned to a heavy 88mm antiaircraft battery in northwest Germany where they ran up against Montgomery's troops.

Author Photo

Owen Kendall (center), a former para trooper of the British 6th Airborne Division joined Schroder and Leithold on their visit to the museum. It was a surprise for him to spot Field Marshal Montgomery's uniform at the Artillery Company Museum in North America. Kendall and a small group of paratroopers overran the German gun positions in April 1945, capturing Schroder among others. Leithold evaded capture and was able to make his way home by travelling nights, avoiding any contact with the advancing Allied armies.

Author Photo

The Artillery Company is always there when a historical military showing is appropriate. The men of the unit can be depended on to answer today's calls to muster quickly, insuring their presence at given exercises as and when required. In addition to such official duty calls, the Company in recent times has offered its services to private groups for legitimate and patriotic purposes. Following are images of activities in which the Artillery Company of Newport participated on private request.

RE

The Artillery Company turned out with an Honor Guard for the wedding of MSGT and Mrs. Elton Colones.

RE

Here, the Artillery Company pulled out one of its historically celebrated Paul Revere cannon to enhance the wishes of the newly weds. Company members set up and closely supervised the igniting of the powder charge for this memorable moment.

RE

Richard Sheffield and Howard Cushing thank COL Robert Edenbach for participating in the May 25, 2013 reopening of Bailey's Beach.

RE

Artillery Company members participating in the dedication of Queen Anne Square are (from left) Mike Pine, Jack Connor, Harry Warner and Robert Edenbach.

APPENDIX I

Charter of 1741

At a General Assembly of His Majesty's Colony of Rhode Island and Providence Plantations, in New England, held by adjournment at South Kingstown, within and for the Colony aforesaid, on the first Monday in February, being the first day of said month, in the fifteenth year of His Majesty's reign, George the Second, King of Great Britain, &c., annoque Domini 1741: -

WHEREAS the preservation of this colony, in time of war, depends, under God, chiefly upon the military skill and discipline of the inhabitants; and it being necessary in order to revive and perpetuate the same, to form and establish a Military Company, which - by acquainting and accustoming themselves to the military exercise, by more frequent training than the body of the people can attend - may serve for a nursery of skillful Officers, and, in time of an actual invasion, by their superior skill and experience, may render the whole Militia more useful and effectual; -

AND WHEREAS a number of the principal inhabitants of the town of Newport - viz, Jahleel Brenton, Godfrey Malbone, Samuel Wickham, Henry Collins, John Gidley, James Honeyman, jun., John Brown, Nataniiel Coddington, jun., Peleg Brown, Charles Bardin, Simon Pease, David Cheeseborough, Philip Wilkinson, John Freebody, jun., Thomas Wickham, Walter Cranston, Sueton Grant, and William Vernon, have freely offered themselves to begin, and with such others as shall be added to them, to form such a Company; and, by their humble Petition, have prayed this Assembly to grant them a Charter, with such privileges and under such restrictions, and limitations as the assembly shall think proper; -

WHEREFORE this Assembly, for the reasons and considerations aforesaid, and in order that all encouragements may be given to the laudable and useful design of the Petitioners, have ordained, constituted, and granted, and by the presented do ordain, constitute, and grant, that they - the said Petitioners, Jaheel Brenton, Godfrey Malbone, Samuel Wickham, Genry Collins, John Gidley, James Honeyman, jum., John Brown, Nataniel Coddington, jun., Peleg Brown, Charles bardin, Simon Pease, David Cheeseborough, Philip Wilinson, John Freebody, jun., Thomas Wickham, Walter Cranston, Sueton Grant, and William Vernon, together with such others as shall be hereafter added to them (not exceeding the number of one hundred in the whole, Officers included) be, and they are hereby declared to be, a Military Company by the name of the ARTILLERY COMPANY OF THE TOWN OF NEWPORT; and by that name they shall have perpetual succession, and shall have and enjoy all the right, powers, and privileges in this grant, hereafter mentioned:

1st, It is granted unto said Company, that they, or the greater number of them, shall and may, once in every year (that is to say, on the last Tuesday in April), meet and assemble themselves together, in some convenient place by them appointed, then and there to choose all other officers; viz, one Captain, two Lieutenants, one Ensign, and all other officers necessary for the training, disciplining, and well chosen but by the greater number of voters then present; the Captain, Lieutenants and Ensign to be approved by the Governor and Council for the time being, and shall be commissioned and engaged in the same manner that other Military Officers in this Colony are.

2nd, That the said Company shall have liberty to meet and exercise themselves upon such other days, and as often, as they shall think necessary, and not be subject to orders or directions of the Colonel or other field officers of the regiment, in whose district they live, in their said meetings and exercises; and that they be obliged to meet for exercising at least four times in a year, upon paying the penalty to and for the use of said Company the following fines: viz., the Captain, for each day's neglect, the sum of five pounds; the Lieutenants and ensign, each forty shillings; the Clerk, the Sergeants, and Corporals, each thirty shillings; - to be levied by a warrant of distress from the Captain or Superior Officer of said Company for the time being, directed to the Clerk.

3rd, That the said Company, or the greater number of them, shall have power to make such rules and orders amongst themselves as they shall think necessary to promote the end of the establishment; and lay such fines and forfeitures upon any of their own Company, for the breach of any such orders and rules, as they shall think proper, so as the same exceed not forty shillings for any one offense; and also shall have full power to levy the said fines and forfeitures which they shall so impose by a warrant of distress from the Captain or Superior Officer of said Company for the time being, directed to the Clerk.

4th, That all those who shall be duly enlisted in this Company, so long as they continue therein, shall be exempted from bearing arms or doing military duty (watching and warding exempted) in the several Companies or trained bands in whose district they respectively belong, except such as shall at the time be Officers in any of the said Companies.

5th, That the Commission Officers of the said Company, from time to time, shall be of the Court Martial and Council of War in the Regiments in whose districts they live.

6th, That if any Officer or Officers of the said Company should be disapproved by the Governor and the council, or should remove out of said town of Newport, or should be taken away by death, - that then , in either of these cases, the Captain of said Company, or the Superior Officer for the time being, shall call the Company together as soon as conveniently may be, and choose others in the room of such Officer or Officers, so disapproved, removed, or taken away by death, in the same manner as heretofore directed.

7th, That the Company, at the time of an alarm, be under the immediate direction of the Captain-General of the Colony; and that the Officers be commissioned accordingly.

(L.S.)

                    SEALED with the seal of the said Colony,
                    by order of the General Assembly

                    James Martin, Secretary

APPENDIX I I

ACN Colonels Commanding

1.	Jahleel Brenton	1741-1747	6 Years
2.	William Mumford	1747-1752	5 Years
3.	Daniel Ayrault Jr.	1752-1771	8 Years
4.	Nathaniel Mumford	1770-1775	5 Years
5.	John Malbone	1775-1792	17 Years
6.	Francis Malbone	1792-1810	18 Years
7.	Benjamin Fry	1810-1815	5 Years
8.	Christopher Grant Champlin	1815-1818	3 Years
9.	Richard Kidder Randolph	1818-1824	6 Years
10.	John B. Lyons	1824-1825	1 Year
11.	Henry Y. Cranston	1825-1828	3 Years
12.	James Boone	1828-1829	1 Year
13	Peleg Clarke	1829-1831	2 Years
14	Nicholas G. Boss	1831-1832	1 Year
15.	Stephen A. Robinson	1832-1837	5 Years
16.	William B. Swan	1837-1845	8 Years
17.	Christopher G.C. Perry	1845-1854	9 Years
18.	Thomas B. Carr	1854-1858	4 Years
19	Charles W. Turner	1858-1860	2 Years
20.	George W. Tew	1860-1862	2 Years
21.	William Stedman	1862-1865	3 Years
22.	John Hare Powel	1865-1877	12 Years
23	Augustus P. Sherman	1877-1879	2 Years
24	George R. Fearing	1879-1882	3 Years
25.	George H. Vaughan	1882-1885	3 Years
26.	Jermiah W. Horton	1885-1891	6 Years
27.	Addison Thomas	1891-1894	3 Years
28.	Alvin A. Barker	1894-1898	4 Years
29.	Henry C. Stevens, Jr.	1898-1899	1 Year
30	Herbert Bliss	1899-1902	3 Years
31.	John D. Richardson	1902-1904	2 Years
32.	Charles L.F. Robinson	1904-1909	5 Years
33.	Frank P. King	1909-1914	5 Years
34.	Arthur A. Sherman	1914-1916	2 Years
35	Robert C. Ebbs	1916-1917	1 Year
36.	Alvin A. Barker	1917-1919	2 Years
37.	William A. Knowe	1919-1920	1 Year
38.	William MacLeod	1920-1921	1 Year
39.	William Knowe	1921-1924	3 Years
40.	Douglas P.A. Jacoby	1924-1929	5 Years
41	Harold E. Knowe	1929-1942	13 Years
42.	Thomas J. Smith	1942-1953	11 Years
43.	Gordon H. Austin	1953-1959	6 Years
44.	Robert Kerr	1960-1961	1 Year
45.	Louis Lorillard	1961-1961	6 months
46.	Harold E. "Zeke" St. John	1961-1964	2 ½ Years
47.	Clen Humphery	1964-1966	2 Years
48.	Robert R. Craft	1966-1968	2 Years
49.	Francis Gauthier	1968-1969	1 Year
50.	John P. Lauth	1969-1973	4 Years
51.	Harold E. "Zeke" St. John	1973-1973	6 months
52.	Frederick T. Kirby	1973-1976	2 ½ Years
53.	Arthur F. Newell	1976-1978	2 ½ Years
54.	Adrien F. Surette	1978-1982	3 Years 7 months
55.	James V. Coleman	1982-1983	1 Year
56.	John Mack	1983-1988	5 Years
57.	Donald E. Norris	1988-1992	4 Years
58.	Frank S. Hale	1992-1996	4 Years
59.	John L.R. Macomber	1996-1997	1 Year 3 months
60.	James R. Johnsen	1997-2000	2 Years 9 months
61.	Roy D. Lauth	2000-2004	4 Years
62.	Geoffrey D. Gardner	2004-2008	4 Years
63.	Robert S. Edenbach Sr	2008-	

APPENDIX III

The Artillery Company Revitalized 1792

(From a 2000 report edited by LTC G. Gardner,
with technical advice by Lt. Douglas Stamford)

Although peace had been declared in 1783, no apparent move was made to reorganize the Artillery Company until July 1792. A group of some 80 subscribers subsequently met for the purpose of forming an Independent Company. Following is the petition presented to the Rhode Island Assembly on August 9th, 1792:

To the Honorable General Assembly, specially convened at Newport, in the County of Newport, on the first Wednesday in August, in the year of our Lord one thousand seven hundred and ninety two.

Respectfully show John Malbone and George Champlin, late Officers in the Artillery Company in the Town of Newport, that said Company was established and a Charter granted them by the General Assembly of the Colony of Rhode Island, in the year of our Lord, one thousand seven hundred and forty one; That said Company continued in the Exercise its Powers therein granted them until the arrival of the British fleet and Army at Newport, in December one thousand seven hundred and seventy six; That by reason thereof the members of said Company were dispersed and no Election of Officers was made from that time until the first of August, one thousand seven hundred and ninety two, when said Company was convened and elected the Officers thereof assigned by the Charter; That doubts having arisen respecting the Right of exercising the Powers therein granted in consequence of a disuse of them during the period aforesaid, for the renewal whereof, the said Company at their said meeting directed an application in a legislative interference. Your petitioners therefore, in their behalf humbly pray that the said Charter may be declared good and effectual for all the purposes therein contained and that the present members of said Company and their successors be empowered to exercise all the Powers therein granted, as fully as if there had been no disuse of the same, and that the Officers elected by said Company held on the said First Day of August, and approved by the Governor and the Council, be the Officers for the said Company agreeable to the Charter.

John Malbone
George Champlin

In Lower House of Assembly 9 August 1792.

Resolved: that the Prayer the within Petition be granted, and that the Charter therein referred to be revived, and the members of said Company enjoy all the privileges which are contained in said Charter.

Voted per Order
Ray Greene, Clerk

In the Upper House,

Read the same day and concurred.

By Order Henry Ward, Secr'y

In the handwriting of Francis Malbone there is this heading to a list of 82 subscribing members of the Artillery Company.

We the Subscribers do hereby acknowledge ourselves duly enlisted into the Artillery Company of the Town of Newport incorporated by an act of the General Assembly passed the 1st Monday in February AD 1741. And do further agree to observe such Rules and Orders as may hereafter be adopted by said Company, Newport 13th August 1792.

APPENDIX IV

Important Dates

1741	Artillery Company chartered February 1 by The General Assembly of His Majesty's (King George II) Colony of Rhode Island and Providence Plantations
1757	1/4 of Company serves in campaign against French forts at Crown Point & Fort William Henry
1776	Captain John Malone surrenders the city of Newport to the British
1777	Col. Campbell and Major Grant killed in action with His Majesties forces in New York
1790	Artillery Company serves as Guard of Honor for General Washington on his visit to Newport
1792	The original Artillery Company Charter is declared 'good' and effective by the Rhode Island General Assembly despite a period of disuse from 1776 to 1792
1812	Members of the Artillery Company serve with Oliver Hazard Perry at the Battle of Lake Erie
1835	Armory Built on Clarke Street on land donated by Audley Clarke
1842	Artillery Company takes position "right of the line" and is instrumental in suppressing the Dorr Rebellion in Providence
1861	Lincoln calls for volunteers and the Artillery Company enlists as Company "F" flag company of the 1st Rhode Island Regiment. Regiment fights 1st Battle of Bull Run and suffers losses
1898	Artillery Company personnel man Fort Adams in war against Spain
1917	Artillery Company volunteers as a unit to serve in Europe under its elected officers. Offer declined by Federal Government. Most members enlist in the A.E.F.
1941	Artillery Company members serve in all theaters of World War II
1950	Artillery Company members serve in Korea
1954 - 1973	Artillery Company members serve in Republic of Vietnam
1992	Artillery Company member flies guidon on his Humvee on entering Kuwait City
2003 - 2006	Artillery Company member serves several tours in Iraq and at Guantanamo Bay

References

Brown, Howard F., COL and Humble, Roberta Mudge, *"The Historic Armories of Rhode Island,"* Pawtucket, Globe Printing, 2000.

Conley, Patrick T. *"Democracy in Decline: Rhode Island's Constitutional Development, 1776-1841."* Providence, RI: Rhode Island Historical Society, 1977.

Conley, Patrick T. *"No Tempest in a Teapot: The Dorr Rebellion in National Perspective."* Rhode Island History 50, 1992.

Conley, Patrick T. *"People, Places, Laws and Lore of the Ocean State,"* A. Rhode Island Historic Sampler, Rhode Island Publications Society, 2012.

Grandchamp, Robert and Lancaster, Jane and Ferguson, Cynthia: *"Rhody Redlegs"*, McFarland, 2012.

McBurney, Christian M. *"The Rhode Island Campaign."* Westholme Publishing, 2011.

Proceedings of a General Court Martial, Holden at Newport, August 1, 1817, for the trial of Captain Robert B. Cranston, of the Newport Artillery.

Gardener, G., LTC, *The Artillery Company Revitalized*, Draft copy 2000. In files of the Artillery Company of Newport.

Hammet, Fred, *The Newport Artillery*, in *The Volunteer*, Vol. 1, No. 6, September 1889.

Kiker, Ruth. *"King George's Yankee Gunners,"*, in Le Bal Rochambeau, Saturday, June 3, 1995.

Unpublished Manuscript by Elton Manuel, dated 1970. In files of the Artillery Company of Newport.

Other Books by the Author

The Hessian Occupation of Newport
and Rhode Island, 1776 - 1779

Stars and Swastikas,
The Boy Who Wore Two Uniforms

Defenses of Narragansett
Bay in WWII

Dutch Island and Fort Greble

Davisville and the Seabees

The Hessian Drummer Boy of Newport

The Author

To date, Walter Schroder has written six books on the subject of military history, with most addressing actions taking place in Rhode Island during the American Revolution and World War II.

In this, his latest book entitled: The Artillery Company of Newport; a pictorial history, he calls the readers' attention to information not generally known beyond the fact that the company is the oldest military unit in Rhode Island still operating under a Charter granted in 1741 by the General Assembly of the British Colony of Rhode Island, which was reconfirmed by Rhode Island's Legislature after the Revolutionary War.

Schroder's unique background, having served with a German anti aircraft artillery unit during the last days of World War II, and the U.S. Army in the ensuing Cold War period, combined with his language skills have enabled him to engage in subject related research of archival materials on both sides of the Atlantic.

He completed a 32-year civilian career with the U.S. Department of Defense and is now retired. In 2007 he was inducted into the Rhode Island Heritage Hall of Fame and continues to use his research and language skills as situations arise. He holds memberships in the Coast Defense Study Group (CDSG), the Council on American's Military Past (CAMP), and is a supporting member of the Artillery Company of Newport and the Fort Adams Trust.

Made in the USA
Charleston, SC
25 January 2014